BRUCE LEE

A Life from Beginning to End

Table of Contents

Introduction

Born in 1940 in San Francisco, Bruce Lee spent his childhood in Hong Kong but became an adult in the United States. Lee brought his memories of the Japanese occupation of Hong Kong, his experiences fighting gangs on the streets, and his ambition for a better life with him on his long journey from east to west. Although driven and ambitious, Lee never excelled academically in the United States. Instead, he chose a different path and did no less than become an international martial arts superstar, breaking down racial prejudice as he did.

By the time *Enter the Dragon*—one of the most popular kung fu movies in history—was released in the United States on July 26, 1973, Bruce Lee had already died. Lee's short life, the many accomplishments he achieved during it, and his mysterious death are tied together in his memory. How could a young man at the peak of physical fitness, an actor whose star was rapidly rising, simply die? But as Lee's wife, Linda Lee Caldwell, said, "All these years later, people still wonder about how Bruce died. I prefer to remember how he lived."

Through his movies, Lee showed the world that a Chinese man could be fiercely proud of his image, more powerful than any white opponent, and be a sex symbol too. From his first feature movie as an adult martial arts star, *Fist of Fury* (1972), to his last, *Game of Death* (1978) released after his death, Lee showed the world something it had never seen before. His on-screen presence was revolutionary.

Off-screen Lee also blazed a new trail in martial arts practice, not only in the United States but around the world. With his signature Jeet Kune Do technique, Lee challenged the authority of traditional forms of martial arts and urged his followers to seek their own truth. His philosophical advice to "be like water" continues to inspire people in all aspects of their life. Lee urged, "Don't get set into one form, adapt it and build your own, and let it grow, be like water. Empty your mind, be formless, shapeless—like water." Following his own advice, Bruce Lee became an icon whose influence continues to adapt and grow, even after death.

Chapter One

Growing Up in Post-War Hong Kong

"There is no such thing as maturity. There is instead an ever-evolving process of maturing."

—Bruce Lee

Bruce Lee entered the world marked with prophetic expectations. Born on November 27, 1940, Lee was a gift of the Chinese zodiac year of the Dragon. The other eleven zodiac symbols are represented by animals; the Dragon is the only symbol that is supernatural. The fifth zodiac sign, the mythic Dragon is believed to represent auspicious power, the gift of good fortune. Those born in the year of the Dragon are said to be potent, powerful, brave, and yet kind.

Although Lee was Chinese, he was born in the United States. His father, Lee Hoi-chuen, was a famous opera singer and was performing in San Francisco at the time of his son's birth. Bruce's mother, Grace Ho, was the adopted daughter of prominent Hong Kong businessman Ho Kom-tong. The Kom-tongs were one of the most powerful clans in Hong Kong, and Lee grew up with the protection of wealth and high status surrounding him.

Grace's biological parentage has been the subject of speculation. It is thought that Grace was multi-racial, with a white European father and Chinese mother. Pregnant with Lee and already the mother of three children, Grace Ho joined her husband on his year-long opera tour of the United States. As a result, Lee entered the world at the Chinese Hospital in San Francisco's Chinatown. The Lee family lived in the U.S. for the first few months of Lee's life before returning to Hong Kong where he remained until he was 18.

Lee's siblings were Phoebe Lee, Agnes Lee, and Peter Lee. The final and fifth child, Robert Lee, was born after Bruce. The name Bruce was not given to Lee by his parents who gave him the traditional Cantonese name Lee Jun-fan. A dubious story about the origin of Lee's name is that the America doctor attending to Lee's birth first referred to him using the English name "Bruce." As the other Lee family children also had English names, the Lee family chose to keep it.

Cantonese naming practices can appear complex to outsiders. Lee had essentially four different names. His birth name, Lee Jun-fan, meant to "return again." Grace had a deep respect for the power of destiny and chose this name because she believed it was Lee's fate to return to the United States. Lee's clan name was Lee Yuen-cham, but he also used Lee Yuen-kam during his studies and Lee Siu-lung as his Chinese screen name. Siu-lung translated to English means "little dragon."

The Lee family's decision to return to Hong Kong in early 1941 was unusual. Many of Lee Hoi-chuen's peers took the opportunity to remain in the United States, where they believed they were safe from the turbulent events taking place in East Asia during World War II. Within months of the family's return to Hong Kong, Japan invaded the region which was a British colony at the time. The governor of Hong Kong officially surrendered the territory to Imperial Japan on December 25, 1941. The Lee family, alongside the one and a half million people of Hong Kong, spent three years and eight months as the colonial subjects of the Empire of Japan. The period of time, three years and eight months, written in Cantonese later became a metonym for the occupation itself.

The Lees lived in the Kowloon district of Hong Kong. Kowloon is located at the southern tip of the Chinese mainland; the now more westernized main island of Hong Kong is accessible from Kowloon via Victoria Harbour. Lee grew up in a two-room apartment above a row of shops at 218 Nathan Road, Kowloon. During the Japanese occupation, a military base was located across the street from the home, and Lee spent hours insulting the forces from his balcony. The oppressive atmosphere of the Japanese occupation kept Bruce at home during his early years. As soon as the British again took control of Hong Kong, Lee jumped at the opportunity to explore his city.

After the Japanese occupation, Lee's father Lee Hoi-chuen was able to restart his career as an opera singer and actor. When he wasn't touring with his opera company, Lee Hoi-chuen rehearsed and performed in music halls and opera houses around Hong Kong. Young Bruce would often go with his father to watch him rehearse. Hanging around the music hall, Lee met another young boy whose father was an actor. Siu Kee Lun, who later adopted the stage name Unicorn, was a few years older than Lee but the pair soon became close friends. It was around this time that

Lee began acting. Introduced to the screen by his father, Lee performed in as many as twenty movies during his childhood and teenage years. His earliest performance took place back in 1941 when he was featured as an infant in *Golden Gate Girl*. From age six, Lee started appearing on screen again, this time in small acting roles for films such as *Sai See in the Dream* (1949), *The Kid* (1950), and *In the Face of Demolition* (1953).

At age 12, Lee began attending La Salle College. A product of his mother's European ancestry, Lee was raised Catholic. Like many young teenagers, Lee bristled against authority and developed a reputation as a troublemaker. Ordinary territorial spats between Chinese boys at La Salle College and European boys at nearby King George V school escalated into street fights that Lee often found himself at the center of. In Hong Kong, street fighting was illegal but common. Lee's acting background, relative wealth, and reputation for trouble made him the target of local gangs. In 1953, aged 13, Lee was badly beaten by a local street gang; an incident later referred to as the first and last time Bruce Lee lost a fight.

Chapter Two

A New Life in America

*"A good martial artist does not become tense, but ready.
Not thinking, yet not dreaming. Ready for whatever may
come. When the opponent expands, I contract; and when he
contracts, I expand. And when there is an opportunity, 'I'
do not hit, 'it' hits all by itself."*

—Bruce Lee

Disturbed by the injuries their son was sustaining from
street fighting, Lee's parents enrolled him in to study
martial arts. Lee began training in Wing Chun-style kung fu
under master Yip Man's tutelage when he was around 15
years old. Under the direction of his father, Lee already
knew the fundamentals of Wu-style t'ai chi chu'an, but it
wasn't until he studied under Yip Man that he began to see
martial arts as his calling. During Lee's classes with Yip
Man, he learned the simple and streamlined nature of Wing
Chun kung fu. Yip Man did not impose any set pattern to
his classes. Instead, he encouraged his students to perform
repetitive *chi sao* (sticking hands) drills and test each other
in free-sparring sessions.

The dangerous streets of post-war Hong Kong were
ruled by street gangs. Yip Man knew that his students had
to navigate these dangerous streets where violence could
erupt at any moment and needed the skills to defend
themselves. But to discourage his students from getting

involved in street fighting, Yip Man organized fighting competitions. Wing Chun emphasized in-fighting at close proximity along an opponent's center line. Students of Wing Chun learned how to use short kicks and rapid punches to overcome their opponents with as little effort as possible.

Although Lee stood out from the other students for his superior speed and precision, he also pursued other interests during these years. In 1954, Lee had begun training as a cha-cha dancer. A dedicated and gifted student, he went on to win the 1958 Hong Kong Crown Colony Cha-Cha Championship. That same year, Lee won the Hong Kong Inter-School Amateur Boxing Championship and starred in the movie *The Orphan* (1958). These many talents Lee later combined and refined to become the world's first martial arts superstar. Yet as a teenager, these talents continued to single Lee out with the local street gangs who he continued to clash with throughout his teens.

Lee was also singled out due to his mixed ancestry. Around a year into Lee's Wing Chun training, the other students learned that his grandfather was a white man and refused to train with him. At one time, traditional Chinese martial artists prohibited teaching their ancestral techniques to non-Asians. This stand-off likely hurt Lee, but he continued to train with Yip Man and another grandmaster Wong Shun Leung. Yip Man rarely taught his students privately. In training one-on-one with Lee, he showed a huge amount of respect for Lee's talent. Lee often sparred with Wong Shun Leung and continued to train with him when they were both living in America.

Although he excelled in the martial arts studio, on the dance floor, in the boxing ring, and on the movie set, Lee continued to struggle in school. The La Salle College Catholic School for boys had expelled Lee in 1956, at the age of 15. The exact reason for his expulsion is unknown, but poor academic performance and poor behavior are likely. Lee enrolled in St. Francis Xavier's College to finish his schooling but never managed to achieve the academic accolades his parents expected.

In the spring of 1959, Lee's frequent violent clashes with street gangs escalated, and his parents grew afraid for his safety. In one fight, Lee allegedly beat up the son of a feared triad family. During another fight the police were called to break it up, and Lee was arrested. His parents feared that their son's reputation and habit of beating up the sons of powerful criminals would get him in serious trouble. If Lee continued down this path, he would either end up in jail or murdered by one of the many organized crime rings then operating in Hong Kong. At the time of Lee's arrest, police warned his parents that they believed there was a contract out on his life. To remove Lee from the dangerous situation he found himself in, his parents arranged for him to move to the United States.

At the age of 18, Lee began a new life in America. He first settled in San Francisco where his older sister, Agnes, was living with friends of the family. After several months Lee moved to Seattle where he studied at Edison Technical School and earned his high school diploma in December 1960. Lee supported himself during these early days in an unfamiliar country by working as a live-in waiter at a Chinese restaurant owned by Ruby Chow. The Chows were family friends of the Lees, and Ruby Chow acted as Lee's American sponsor.

It's safe to say, however, that Lee did not enjoy his time working at the restaurant. Inefficient as a waiter, he is said to have had a bad attitude and treat customers and colleagues with hostility. Ruby Chow has said of Lee, "He was just not the sort of person you want your children to grow up like—he was wild and undisciplined, he had no respect." Undoubtedly, Lee struggled to adjust to his life in Seattle and spent as much of his spare time as he could developing his martial arts skills.

Lee enrolled at the University of Washington in March of 1961 where he majored in drama and also studied philosophy and psychology. Academia was not Lee's strong suit, and by March of 1962, one year into his studies, he was floundering with a 1.84 GPA. During his college years, Lee focused his attention on opening his own martial arts studios rather than writing essays for his classes. That's not to say he didn't write. While Lee was still a student he wrote his first book, *Chinese Gung Fu: The Philosophical Art of Self-Defense*. This book includes photographs of combat moves shot in the parking lot of Ruby Chow's restaurant. Lee was a prolific writer who filled spiral notebooks with diagrams and descriptions of fight scenarios.

It was also during Lee's time at the University of Washington that he met his future wife, Linda Emery. Lee was teaching martial arts to students at the university and met Linda when she became one of his pupils. Linda and Lee were married on August 17, 1964.

Chapter Three

The One-Inch Punch

"Adapt what is useful, reject what is useless, and add what is specifically your own."

—Bruce Lee

From his arrival in San Francisco in 1959, Lee developed and taught his own unique brand of martial arts named Jun Fan Gung Fu meaning "Bruce Lee's kung fu." San Francisco already had its own martial arts scene centered in the city's Chinatown district. Yet the martial arts culture in San Francisco operated very differently to the one Lee knew in Hong Kong.

San Francisco's Chinatown is the oldest Chinese community in North America. Established in 1848 when the first Chinese immigrants arrived on a sailing vessel, San Francisco's Chinatown is a thriving hub of Chinese culture. Residents of Chinatown established their own kung fu culture in the 1930s with the opening of Hung Sing, the first public martial arts school in America. The school was presided over by kung fu masters Lau Bun and T.Y. Wong.

Both Lau Bun and his junior T.Y. Wong encouraged the young men of Chinatown to adhere to a strict code of conduct. Street fighting, common on the streets of Hong Kong, was forbidden in Chinatown. The two men also recruited their students to act as unofficial security around Chinatown's Forbidden City nightclub. T.Y. Wong opened his own martial arts school in the early 1940s and named it Kin Mon, meaning the "Sturdy Citizen's Club."

In Chinatown, those who had practiced Wing Chun kung fu in Hong Kong had a reputation. Wing Chun was an economical, results-oriented style, an important feature for young men used to fighting on the streets of post-war Hong Kong. Yet it wasn't this difference in style but a difference in attitude that first caused the clash between Lau Bun and Bruce Lee.

When Lee first arrived in San Francisco, he went to Hung Sing to check out the competition. Intending to introduce himself and demonstrate his superior skills, Lee offended the Hung Sing masters. Lee's insistence that Wing Chun was the ultimate martial arts style and that traditional styles taught in Chinatown schools were ineffective came across as arrogance, and he was told to leave the Hung Sing School and never come back.

Lee's criticism of the established kung fu scene in Chinatown was both vocal and published. In Lee's book *Chinese Gung Fu*, he challenges techniques put forth in one of T.Y. Wong's books in an unsubtle photo-by-photo comparison. Lee refers to traditional martial arts forms taught by masters like T.Y. Wong and Lau Bun as "slower . . . half-cultivated systems." These comments infuriated Chinatown's martial arts community, and Lee was shunned by masters and students alike.

Lee opened his own martial arts studio, the Lee Jun Fan Gung Fu Institute in Seattle, in 1960. Taky Kimura was hired to be Lee's assistant instructor, and Kimura continued to teach the techniques of Lee Jun Fan Gung Fu after Lee's death.

Within a few years after opening his studio, Lee was ready for a change. In October of 1964, Linda was pregnant with the couple's first child, and Lee decided to drop out of college and move to Oakland. In Oakland, Lee moved in with James Yimm Lee, a martial artist twenty years his senior. James had a reputation as a street fighter in his youth and was running a modern martial arts training school out of his garage.

Together, Lee and James established the second Lee Jun Fan Gung Fu Institute in Oakland. Finally, Lee was part of a progressive martial arts community where he could develop his techniques with like-minded collaborators. To promote this school, Lee performed demonstrations of his unique fighting style in front of audiences of hundreds. During these demonstrations, Lee took the opportunity to criticize his peers. Referring to the San Francisco's Chinatown martial artists as "dry-land swimmers," Lee performed moves in the Northern Shaolin style before tearing them apart and explaining why they would never work in a real fight.

Lee delivered one of these scathing lectures at Ed Parker's first Long Beach International Karate Tournament in August 1964. First Lee impressed the crowd by performing two-finger push-ups and his legendary one-inch punch. Bob Baker, the volunteer that allowed Lee to perform the one-inch punch on him, said of the event, "When he punched me that last time, I had to stay home from work because the pain in my chest was unbearable."

It was at this time that the legendary rivalry between Lee and Wong Jack Man reached its climax. Wong Jack Man had arrived on the San Francisco Chinatown martial arts scene around the same time Lee's controversial book was published. The first martial artist to fight in an elegant northern style in Chinatown, Wong Jack Man impressed the old guard who were themselves devotees of southern Shaolin. Wong's fighting style was the inverse of Lee's. Where Wing Chun was a form of economical, close-range combat, Wong's northern style was typified by long-range attacks delivered in elegant, acrobatic moves.

A few weeks after his performance at the Long Beach Tournament, Lee spoke before a huge crowd at the Sing Sing Theatre in San Francisco's Chinatown. This time, Lee took his criticism of Chinatown martial artists even further, disrespecting community elders Lau Bun and T.Y. Wong by saying "these old tigers have no teeth." Lee also lay down a challenge, declaring that he could beat anyone in San Francisco. A confrontation was inevitable.

Chapter Four

Fight with Wong Jack Man

"There are no limits. There are plateaus, but you must not stay there, you must go beyond them. If it kills you, it kills you. A man must constantly exceed his level."

—Bruce Lee

Wong Jack Man challenge to Lee came in the form of a letter. The letter was hand-delivered by David Chin at Lee's martial arts studio in Oakland. Penned by the Gee Yau Seah martial arts academy, the letter expressed irritation at Lee's performance at the Sing Sing Theatre a few days before. Some members of Gee Yau Seah had been at the theatre that night and heard every boastful slur Lee had made. Lee made it clear during his demonstration that no-one in San Francisco was a match for his superior skills. Wong Jack Man begged to differ. Lee laughed and found the materials to pen a letter of his own, happily accepting Wong's challenge to fight.

It was not the first time that Lee had risen to a challenge. In Seattle a few years earlier, another martial arts practitioner had taken issue with Lee's disrespect towards traditional martial art forms. Yoichi Nakachi, a Seattle karate teacher, publicly challenged Lee to a fight. Eventually, the pair came to blows, and Lee destroyed Nakachi in a vicious fight said to have lasted a mere eleven seconds. Landing his powerful punches in the right spots,

Lee disarmed Nakachi and struck his head with a blow that made him lose consciousness and fractured his skull.

Now Lee insisted that his fight with Wong take place in his Oakland studio. So one evening in the late autumn of 1964, Wong got into a car with five other men and drove from Chinatown to Broadway Avenue in Oakland. Among the men were David Chin and Chan Keung, two martial artists from the Ghee Yau Seah School. The other three men weren't part of the martial arts community but knew they could regale their friends with stories of this fight for years to come. Notably, no student of T.Y. Wong's Kin Mon or Lau Bun's Hung Sing school had anything to do with the planned spat. Abiding by the strict code of conduct enforced by Lau Bun, these students kept their distance from the trouble.

As soon as the Wong party arrived at Lee's studio and Lee locked the front door, it became clear that Wong did not know what he had gotten himself into. Wong was approaching the fight as a sparring match, a traditional show of strength in the spirit of a demonstration. Lee saw the fight differently. Drawing on his experience fighting gangs on the streets of Hong Kong, Lee was prepared to fight to the death. Lee's friend and associate James Yimm Lee even had a loaded handgun with him in case the fight got out of hand.

The fight between Bruce Lee and Wong Jack Man is something of an urban legend. With only a handful of witnesses—Wong's five associates, Lee's wife Linda, and James Yimm Lee—accounts of the fight vary. The most often repeated account starts with Lee lashing out before the two men had even finished shaking hands. Lee rushed at Wong with extreme aggression, striking Wong's head with a blow that cut his forehead. Wong told friends he would avoid kicking Lee because he didn't want to cause permanent injury, but Lee pummeled Wong with a series of groin kicks and close punches.

It's said that Wong had Lee in a headlock at one point but chose not to strike him in that position, fearing he could mortally injure him and end up in jail. The fight was crude, and the men thrashed around the room for five minutes or more. Eventually, Wong stumbled and fell to the ground giving Lee the opportunity to strike him from above. Lee shouted for Wong to yield in Cantonese over and over. According to David Chin, Wong conceded, and they stopped the fight. Chin said, "The whole thing lasted . . . not more than seven minutes."

Some say the fight between Lee and Wong took place because Lee insisted on teaching kung fu to non-Chinese students. In this telling of events, the established martial arts community in Chinatown took umbrage at Lee's inclusive teaching stance. To warn Lee, they sent Wong to his studio to demonstrate their displeasure. This theory forms part of the storyline in the movie *Dragon: The Bruce Lee Story*, but there is little evidence to support it. Both T.Y. Wong and Lau Bun taught non-Chinese students as did other less senior students opening schools in Chinatown in the 1960s.

When the fight was over, speculation on what had taken place behind that locked door went into overdrive. According to some witnesses the fight lasted an unrealistic 20-25 minutes and there was no true victor, just a very winded Lee and a bruised Wong. Both men agreed not to talk or write about the fight, but Lee broke his silence when he agreed to give an interview in a Chinese language newspaper. A different newspaper had published a story in which they accused Lee and Wong of fighting over the affections of actress Zhang Zhongwen. Zhongwen had once been Lee's cha-cha partner, and Lee wanted to refute any suggestion of her involvement.

Wong was unhappy with Lee's version of events and published his own account in San Francisco's *Pacific Weekly* newspaper. Urban legend holds that Wong called for a rematch in this article. The actual text reads, "(Wong) says that in the future he will not argue his case again in the newspaper, and if he is made to fight again, he will instead hold a public exhibition so that everyone can see with their own eyes." Lee chose not to rise to the bait and instead to focus on his school, his family, and restarting his acting career.

Chapter Five

Jeet Kune Do, the Way of the Intercepting Fist

"Empty your mind, be formless. Shapeless, like water. If you put water into a cup, it becomes the cup. You put water into a bottle and it becomes the bottle. You put it in a teapot, it becomes the teapot. Now, water can flow or it can crash. Be water, my friend."

—Bruce Lee

Lee's messy victory over Wong influenced his move away from Wing Chun towards his own hybrid martial arts system, Jeet Kune Do. Lee had proclaimed the superiority of Wing Chun since his arrival in San Francisco, but his pride took a hit during his fight with Wong, who proved himself a worthy adversary. Lee told Linda he was disappointed the fight had lasted so long. Whether the fight lasted twenty minutes or seven minutes, it took Lee far longer to dominate Wong than the eleven seconds it took to destroy Nakachi.

Lee developed a martial arts system that was eclectic rather than restrictive. The style of no style, Jeet Kune Do, which translates to "the way of the intercepting fist," was more than a martial art, it was a philosophy for life. He used techniques common in boxing, fencing, and other forms of exercise and adapted them to suit each student's needs. Lee himself also started weight training to build up strength and running to improve endurance. The focus of Jeet Kune Do was practicality and efficiency, the ability to overcome one's opponent as quickly as possible.

Jeet Kune Do was Lee's way of freeing his followers from the existing kung fu forms and institutions. He did not envisage Jeet Kune Do as an organized institution but as "a mirror in which to see ourselves." For Lee, the simplest way was the right way, and in his martial arts he sought to express himself with minimal movements and a low expenditure of energy. The philosophy of Jeet Kune Do is one of openness and receptivity, and its core belief is that the truth only exists outside all molds and patterns. Awareness is never exclusive.

One of Lee's favorite Zen stories was that of the teacup. The story begins with a learned man approaching a Zen teacher for instruction. The teacher starts sharing his philosophies, but the man interrupts to point out where their teachings agrees or differs. In response the Zen teacher fills the man's teacup until it overflows and stops only when the man cries out, "Enough!" The teacher then asks the man, "If you do not first empty your cup, how can you taste my tea?" On this topic, Bruce Lee said, "In order to taste my cup of water you must first empty your cup. My friend, drop all your preconceived and fixed ideas and be neutral. Do you know why this cup is useful? Because it is empty."

Of Jeet Kune Do, Lee wrote, "Again let me remind you Jeet Kune Do is just a name used, a boat to get one across, and once across it is to be discarded and not to be carried on one's back." Lee wrote time and time again of his philosophy of casting off that which is useless and working towards creating a martial art composed of bare combat essentials.

Having experienced his fair share of fights both in Hong Kong and now in America, Lee insisted that Jeet Kune Do be effective in real combat. Lee claimed that flashy and flowery kung fu techniques were not practical. Geared more towards tournament wins and accolades, these systems would not have an impact in a real street fight. According to Lee, traditional kung fu techniques fooled their practitioners into thinking they were skilled fighters, but they would be easily defeated by fighters willing to use any means necessary to win. Key to Jeet Kune Do is the ability to adapt to the constant changes of real combat with a living, breathing opponent.

As seen in his iconic clash with Chuck Norris in *The Way of the Dragon* (1972), Lee fought in a side southpaw horse stance. Diverging from Muay Thai's signature check, Lee used an oblique leg kick to block, and his jabs and crosses came from his right. Lee's footwork is often remarked upon as he displayed a skippy, nimble style, adapted from Muhammad Ali's boxing stance. Some of the most recognizable principles of Jeet Kune Do are its punches. The straight lead punch is not a power strike but a loose and easy punch designed for speed. The non-telegraphic punch is an explosive hit that offers its opponent no warning signs and is an essential part of the art of June Keet Do.

One of Lee's most famous quotes is "Be like water." To achieve whatever it is you wish to achieve, you must be fluid and adaptable. Water is shapeless, and when put into a receptacle it becomes that receptacle. If you put water into a cup, Lee said, it becomes the cup. The key to Jeet Kune Do is the ability to adapt to any given situation and find the appropriate action within yourself. Only by being like water can you absorb new knowledge and achieve your best in life and combat.

The diversity of Jeet Kune Do's combat style was revolutionary. Lee's students trained in kicking, punching, trapping, and grappling in equal measure at a time when most fighting systems focused on just one or two of these things. These four ranges of combat were later embraced by the mixed martial arts (MMA) community.

Chapter Six

Making it in the Movies

"To hell with circumstances; I create opportunities."

—Bruce Lee

Lee wanted to return to his acting career in America but soon realized he would have to overcome endemic institutional racism to do so. At the time, Chinese actors in America were sometimes cast in small parts as servants, warlords, or opium pushers but never in mainstream movies as complex protagonists. Even if, on rare occasions, a movie required an Asian actor for a leading role, the part would go to a white actor wearing makeup.

By this point, Linda Lee had given birth to a son, Brandon, and Bruce was trying to support his family through his martial art school. Back in 1964, Lee had been introduced to television producer William Dozier who wanted to cast him in a TV show. After auditioning for a show called *Number One Son* that was never made, Lee won the role of Kato, sidekick to the title character of *The Green Hornet*. *The Green Hornet* ran for one season between September 1966 and March 1967 before being canceled. Lee picked up a few small parts in other Dozier-produced TV shows over the next year but struggled to find other acting roles.

For a time Lee focused on working behind the scenes in the movie industry and gave martial arts tuition people like

Roman Polanski and Steve McQueen. He also choreographed fight scenes for *The Wrecking Crew* (1969) starring Dean Martin and Sharon Tate and *A Walk in the Spring Rain* (1970) with Ingrid Bergman. In 1971, Lee was still unable to find a role for himself on television so he decided to write his own. *The Warrior* was a TV series starring a Shaolin fighter in the Old West who battled cowboys without the use of guns. Lee pitched this show to Warner Brothers who resisted giving the lead role to a Chinese actor, blaming their decision on Lee's "thick accent." Soon after, Warner Brothers launched a show called *Kung Fu* that had a very similar concept to *The Warrior*. David Carradine was cast in the role of the Shaolin fighter.

Frustrated by the lack of opportunity in Hollywood, Lee made the decision to return to Hong Kong in 1971. By this time, the Lees had two children, Brandon who was born in 1965 and Shannon, born in 1969. Unknown to Lee, *The Green Hornet* was released in Hong Kong and had proved a massive success. In Hong Kong, the series was even marketed as *The Kato Show*, giving Lee huge exposure and popularity. On the back of *The Kato Show*, Lee was now a household name in Hong Kong and as soon as he arrived was able to negotiate with major production companies, Shaw Brothers and Golden Harvest.

In 1971, Lee signed a contract with Golden Harvest to develop and star in two martial arts movies. The first movie Bruce Lee made with Golden Harvest was *The Big Boss* (1971). The U.S. distributor changed the name of this movie to *Fists of Fury,* which may have been the result of a mix-up. The second movie Lee made in Hong Kong was

Fist of Fury (1972) in Chinese so the American distributor changed the name of this second movie to *The Chinese Connection*. Both movies were huge hits at the Chinese box office. The records set by these two movies were only beaten by Lee's third movie, *The Way of the Dragon* (1972). Lee wrote, directed, produced, and starred in *The Way of the Dragon*; he read dozens of books every aspect of movie making to prepare himself for the task.

Lee had met American karate champion Chuck Norris at a 1964 demonstration in Long Beach, California. He needed a worthy opponent to fight against in the movie's iconic final death scene and chose Norris for the part. Initially, producers offered the role to karate champion Joe Lewis who turned it down. Lee had Norris gain weight for the role of Colt and spent more than 45 hours filming the fight scene between them. Set in Rome, Italy, *The Way of the Dragon* is considered one of the most memorable martial arts movies of all time.

The Way of the Dragon confirmed Lee's status, not only as a martial arts superstar but as a movie sex symbol. Representing a new kind of Asian masculinity, Lee was strong and fierce. The way Lee used his body in his astonishing fight scenes mirrored the way musical actors like Fred Astaire would perform their physical virility on screen. Like these Hollywood giants who controlled every aspect of their performance, Lee controlled not only his own choreography but the entire movie making process. In the 1970s, Lee's authorship over his own image showed him to be years ahead of his time.

Chapter Seven

Enter the Dragon

"Art reaches its greatest peak when devoid of self-consciousness. Freedom discovers man the moment he loses concern over what impression he is making or about to make."

—Bruce Lee

In 1972, Bruce Lee was the biggest box office star in Hong Kong history. Lee's on-screen persona appealed to both Chinese and Western audiences, and it was only a matter of time before Hollywood realized its earlier mistake. The time was right for Lee's crossover from Hong Kong to America, and he knew it. Speaking to the American press, Lee compared his martial arts movies to the James Bond franchise in their treatment of humor and violence. When Lee received his invitation to Hollywood it was in the form of a collaboration between Warner Brothers and Golden Harvest to finance a new Bruce Lee movie.

In August 1972, Lee had begun working on a fourth movie with Golden Harvest titled *The Game of Death*. Once the offer from Warner Brothers was finalized in November 1972, production of *The Game of Death* stopped, and Lee began work on his new movie, *Enter the Dragon*.

The Chinese title of *Enter the Dragon* is *Long Zheng Hu Dou*, which translates to "Struggling dragon, fighting tiger." In Chinese culture this phrase refers to a battle between equal forces. The opening sequence of *Enter the Dragon* sees Lee dominate Sammo Hung in front of a gathering of Shaolin monks. After Lee confirms his Jeet Kune Do philosophy and deep spiritual insight with one of the monks, a British investigator arrives to ask Lee for a favor.

Lee must take down a Shaolin disciple turned villain, Han. Lee's task is to infiltrate Han's martial arts tournament, find the information the authorities need to arrest him, and then return. The British investigator answers Lee's question about why they don't just shoot the man with a traditional wuxia response, "Any idiot can pull a trigger." The final showdown between Lee and Han takes place in a room of mirrors, a cinematic trope repeated many times since. It's unclear who is the struggling dragon and who is the fighting tiger in this scenario. Han, like all good villains, has a prosthetic hand that is outfitted with metal claws. Lee's only weapons are his hands and feet, which he uses to defeat Han once and for all.

Enter the Dragon (1973) remains the highest-grossing martial arts movie of all time. The movie was produced with an estimated budget of $850,000 and grossed $90 million in the global box office, $25 million of which was in the United States. The success of *Enter the Dragon* made Golden Harvest the leading martial arts movie production company in the world. Shaw Brothers, Golden Harvest's main competitors, were pushed out of the martial arts market. Golden Harvest then secured contracts with Sammo Hung and Jackie Chan, both of whom had small roles in *Enter the Dragon*.

With *Enter the Dragon*, Lee introduced Western audiences to strong Chinese lead characters proud of their Asian heritage. Mirroring the effect *Shaolin Temple* (1982) later had on the youth of mainland China, *Enter the Dragon* sparked a martial arts frenzy in the United States. Dojos began popping up all over California and spread quickly to other parts of the country. Kung fu movies became a regular slot on the screening schedules of movie theatres. Newer martial arts practitioners embraced Lee's concept of Jeet Kune Do, and this phenomenon later led to the emergence of MMA.

Before the shooting of *Enter the Dragon* was even finished, it was clear to everyone that Lee was on the cusp of international super stardom. Lee received offers to star in numerous movies and TV shows alongside stars like Elvis and Sophia Loren. But fame has its downsides. Lee was hounded by the Hong Kong press and found himself under pressure to live up to the hype that surrounded him. Early in the filming for *Enter the Dragon*, Lee had a severe anxiety attack on set. This sudden decline in Lee's mental health put principal shooting on hold for two weeks, a long delay for a shooting schedule. Lee also developed a nervous facial tick during filming that the cinematographers struggled to shoot around.

As Lee's life became more intense, so too did his diet and training. Fitness and nutrition were always key parts of Lee's martial arts training. After his fight with Wong Jack Man, Lee intensified his workout regime and carved out the incredible physique for which he became renowned. He followed a strict diet to maintain his fitness, avoiding refined flour and baked goods and following a typical

Asian diet of rice, vegetables, and fish. During filming, Lee stepped it up a notch and ate only raw vegetables and protein shakes that he made from raw beef mince, eggs, and milk, causing his weight to drop from his standard 140lbs to 120lbs. By the time filming for *Enter the Dragon* ended, Lee's friends were concerned about his health.

Chapter Eight

Health Issues and Sudden Death

"A goal is not always meant to be reached, it often serves as something to aim at."

—Bruce Lee

On May 10, 1973, *Enter the Dragon* was entering the final stages of production. Lee was working in a dubbing studio at Golden Harvest in Hong Kong when he began to feel unwell. Lee collapsed in seizures, and when he awoke he complained of a bad headache. Colleagues rushed Lee to Hong Kong Baptist Hospital where he briefly slipped into a coma. Doctors diagnosed cerebral edema, or swelling of the brain, as the cause of Lee's collapse and prescribed the drug mannitol. The swelling subsided, and Lee was discharged from hospital. In the weeks and months after this incident, Lee returned to life as normal—or as normal as it could be at that time. Lee was in the early days of international fame that was causing him extreme stress.

On July 20, 1973, Lee spent the day with his wife, Linda. He had plans to meet with his producer Raymond Chow and actor George Lazenby that evening. It is thought that Lee wanted to persuade Lazenby to appear in his next movie, *The Game of Death*, the shooting of which had been pushed back for *Enter the Dragon*.

Before his meeting, Lee went to the apartment of Betty Ting Pei, a young Taiwanese actress. Betty was a little know actress who performed in small parts in comedies and musicals. On the evening of July 20, Lee and Betty were going over the script for *The Game of Death*, in which she was to have a part. Lee complained of a headache, and Betty gave him an aspirin-based painkiller and told him to lie down in her bed. The painkiller, Equagesic, was something Betty used herself on a regular basis. After taking the drug, Lee went to sleep and never woke up. When Betty could not wake him up for his dinner appointment with Raymond Chow, she called an ambulance. A doctor arrived and attempted to resuscitate Lee before rushing him to the Queen Elizabeth Hospital. Lee was declared dead on arrival, aged 32.

Following Lee's death, an exhaustive nine-day coroner's inquest was held. The cause of death was declared as "misadventure," meaning it was an accident. Lee had died from cerebral edema caused by hypersensitivity to an ingredient in the drug Equagesic. According to the autopsy report, Lee's brain was significantly swollen (a mass increase of 13%), and Equagesic was found in his system.

In recent years, there has been speculation in the press that this cause of death is not accurate. A doctor working at the Cook County medical examiner's office in Chicago has suggested that rather than dying from a reaction to drugs, Lee died from a condition related to epilepsy. Sudden Unexpected Death in Epilepsy (SUDEP) is a rare condition that was first recognized in 1995. SUDEP causes a seizure which can stop the heart or the lungs and is the cause of death for thousands of people every year.

After Lee's death, his wife Linda returned to Seattle where she had his body buried at Lake View Cemetery. Chuck Norris, Taky Kimura, Steve McQueen, James Coburn, George Lazenby, Dan Inosanto, Peter Chin, and Robert Lee were Bruce Lee's pallbearers.

Enter the Dragon was released in Hong Kong on July 26, 1973, six days after Lee's death and became a huge success. *The Game of Death*, the movie Lee was gathering actors for on the day he died, was eventually released in 1978. Robert Clouse directed *The Game of Death* and made the controversial move of finishing the movie using a Bruce Lee lookalike, Kim Tai Chung, and a stunt double. Lee had shot around 100 minutes of footage for *The Game of Death* before his death of which fifteen minutes made it into the final cut.

Lee was at the beginning of what was set to become a long and fruitful career in the movies. He wrote his own scripts and was working on several projects before he died. Raymond Chow at Golden Harvest wanted Lee to star in a movie called *Yellow-Faced Tiger* directed by Lo Wei, and Lee was scheduled to perform in a Shaw Brothers period movie called *The Seven Sons of the Jade Dragon*. None of these projects were ever realized.

Chapter Nine

Theories Surrounding Lee's Death

"All these years later, people still wonder about how Bruce died. I prefer to remember how he lived."

—Linda Lee Caldwell

Bruce Lee's death came as an incredible shock to those who knew him and the fans who were just getting to know him on screen. No-one could believe that a young man at the peak of physical fitness could die from taking a single painkiller. In an attempt to make sense of a senseless tragedy, people turned to alternative theories about how and why Bruce Lee died.

During Lee's autopsy, medical examiners found trace amounts of cannabis in his system. This led to wild speculation that illicit narcotics played some role in Lee's death. However, the forensic scientist assigned to Lee's case made it clear that the small amount of cannabis had nothing to do with Lee's collapse or death. The clinical pathologist at Queen Elizabeth Hospital where Lee was pronounced dead also reported that cannabis played no role in Lee's death.

Chuck Norris fueled speculation that Lee took drugs other than Equagesic when he spoke at the 1975 Comic-Con convention. Norris said that Lee had ruptured a disc in his back in 1968 during a weight-lifting accident. To treat this pain, Lee took muscle-relaxant medication. This rumor was given further credence in the 2017 episode of *Autopsy: The Last Hours of...* that covered Bruce Lee's death. In this episode, forensic pathologist Dr. Michael Hunter suggests Lee died of an adrenal crisis brought on by misuse of cortisone, an anti-inflammatory medication.

Another theory surrounding Lee's death is that he was killed by assassins. In this scenario, Lee had offended some sect of Chinese triads because he refused to pay them for protection. In response, they had him assassinated. Either Betty Ting Pei was in on this triad plot or an unknown person planted the drugs that caused Lee's cerebral edema and killed him.

This theory was given new life in 2009 when actor David Carradine died in a hotel room in Bangkok. Carradine's body was found naked with a rope tied around his neck, wrists, and genitals leading some to assume his death was the result of a sex act gone wrong. Yet the Carradine family attorney suggested that Carradine was killed for trying to uncover secret groups working in the martial arts underworld, the same groups that some claim had a hand in Lee's death. There is no evidence to support this claim.

Some believe that Lee's death was the result of bad feng shui. Feng shui is a Chinese system of thought. Based on the belief that humans can control the flow of energy through space, feng shui involves arranging architectural elements and objects according to specific laws. Many Chinese people hire a feng shui practitioner when they move into a new home to arrange furniture to have a positive effect on their life. Chinese architects may also hire a geomancer to ensure their building design adheres to the tenets of good feng shui. After Lee's death, the Chinese press speculated that bad omens had foretold the star's demise.

Typhoon Dot hit Hong Kong in July of 1973, one day before Lee's death. The typhoon winds knocked down a tree at Lee's home and blew his *pat kwe* (an octagonal wooden-framed mirror said to deflect bad energy) from the roof. In the absence of his *pat kwe*, Lee is said to have become vulnerable to poor fortune. Of course, Bruce died at the home of Betty Ting Pei, not in his own apartment. According to some, Betty Ting Pei's home also suffered from bad feng shui as it was located in the Kowloon Tong area of Hong Kong, an area known to be geographically inauspicious.

One of the most enduring conspiracy theories surrounding Lee's death is that he was the victim of a curse that later took his son Brandon Lee's life. Brandon was eight years old when his father died. As an adult, Brandon decided to follow in his father's footsteps and become an actor. Brandon's lineage and his father's training opened doors for him in Hollywood, and in his first acting gig he starred alongside David Carradine in a made-for-tv kung fu movie. In 1991, Brandon performed in *Showdown in Little Tokyo* alongside Dolf Lundgren. In 1993, Brandon was 28 years old and ready to make his bid for stardom.

Brandon took the lead role in *The Crow*, a dark fantasy movie based on a comic book. This was a massive change of direction from the low budget kung fu and action movies Brandon had made before. On March 31, 1993, there were just eight days left of shooting on *The Crow*. Brandon was ready to shoot the scene in which his character is murdered by a local gangster. The director called action, and Brandon walked into the shot where the gangster was holding a gun loaded with a blank. The gangster shot the gun and Brandon went down, exactly as planned.

But after the director called cut and Brandon did not get up, it became clear that something had gone terribly wrong. The gun that was supposed to hold a blank actually held a blank with the lead tip of a bullet, used in an earlier close-up scene, lodged in front of it. The lead tip tore into Brandon's abdomen leaving a huge hole. Brandon lost a lot of blood, and after 13 hours of surgery and blood transfusions he died in hospital.

The shooting was ruled as accidental, the result of massive on-set negligence. While some have suggested that Chinese triads had a hand in Brandon's death or that supernatural forces were at play, in reality Brandon died because of cost-cutting measures taken on the movie set. Instead of purchasing commercial dummy cartridges, the prop crew had created their own by altering live rounds, unknowingly causing Brandon's fatal accident.

Chapter Ten

Bruce Lee's Legacy

"The doubters said,
'Man can not fly,'
The doers said,
'Maybe, but we'll try,'
And finally soared
In the morning glow
While non-believers
Watched from below."

—Bruce Lee

Lee's book *Tao of Jeet Kune Do* was published in 1975. He had begun writing this text in 1970 after suffering a back injury while weightlifting. To allow his injury to heal, Lee was advised to cease training and wear a back brace for six months. During his difficult convalescence, Lee attempted to get his philosophy and approach to martial arts down on paper. He wrote the bulk of his treatise in one session but added to his notes with other disparate thoughts and ideas in the years leading up to his death. After Lee's death, Linda decided to collect Lee's writings and publish them. Linda hired Gilbert L. Johnson to be the principal editor and used the help of Lee's students to organize the material into an order that made sense.

First editions and special-run hardback editions of *Tao of Jeet Kune Do* are highly desirable to collectors, as are the teaching skills of the only three instructors Lee personally certified. One of these instructors, Dan Inosanto, holds the 3rd rank in Jeet Kune Do, Jun Fan Gung Fu, and Tao of Chinese Gung Fu. The other two certified instructors are Taky Kimura and James Yimm Lee (who died in December of 1972). Ted Wong, who was certified 2nd rank in Jeet Kune Do, was made an instructor by Inosanto, the only person given that position after Lee's death.

Lee urged his instructors to keep the number of students attending their schools low as a way of keeping the quality high. After his death, his instructors kept his two kung fu schools open, and Inosanto continued to teach Jeet Kune Do for the next thirty years. Inosanto certified hundreds of students during this time, keeping Lee's martial art legacy alive.

Today, Lee is a national hero in China, although it took a long time for the Chinese people to celebrate Lee in the same way as the rest of the world. Breaking down racial prejudices by presenting the world with an image of Chinese masculinity that was powerful, successful, and attractive, Lee was a symbol of Chinese nationalism. During Chairman Mao's reign, however, Lee's movies were banned by China's communist government as spiritual pollution. It wasn't until Hong Kong was returned by the United Kingdom to China in 1997 that the relationship between the communist mainland and the capitalist island thawed. In 2008, China state TV produced and aired a 50-part documentary on Bruce Lee's life in an attempt to reclaim their famous son.

Lee was fiercely proud of his Chinese heritage. His ancestral home is located in Jun'an village, which is part of Shunde district in Foshan, Guangdong Province. In 2006, a Bruce Lee theme park was built in Shunde. Known in English as "Bruce Lee Paradise", the theme park is set over 3,000 acres and features the largest Bruce Lee statue in the world.

Hong Kong has also taken steps to preserve Lee's heritage. Hong Kong's heritage museum launched a five-year exhibition called "Bruce Lee: Kung Fu, Art, Life" celebrating Lee's achievements on the 40th anniversary of his death in 2013. The exhibition was so popular that its run was extended until 2020. One of the most famous tourist attractions in Hong Kong is the memorial statue of Lee located on the Avenue of Stars, Tsim Sha Tsui. The statue is bronze and depicts Lee in his classic standing pose, ready to strike. Unveiled in November 2005, on what would have been Lee's 65th birthday, the statue was funded by the Rubão Fan Club in honor of Bruce Lee's legacy.

Lee's impact on the history of cinema should not be underestimated. The kung fu mania of the early seventies was a direct response to the popularity of Lee's movies. In the years following his death, filmmakers in Hong Kong and the United States tried to cash in by churning out forgettable low-budget martial arts movies. These movies did have a positive effect as they launched the careers of other Asian stars such as Jackie Chan. American actor Chuck Norris also became a huge star thanks to a run of 1980s Western martial arts movies that would not have been made if it wasn't for the success of *Enter the Dragon*.

In 1984, huge box office hit *The Karate Kid* featured a heavy dose of Eastern philosophy packaged in a typical Western underdog story. Then in 1988, Jean-Claude Van Damme starred in *Bloodsport*, a movie whose storyline is similar to *Enter the Dragon*. In the 1990s, Hong Kong cinema entered its Golden Age but struggled to find new talent when stars such as Jet Li, Jackie Chan, and choreographer Yuen Woo-ping made the transition to Hollywood. The Wachowski brothers took the ingenious step of hiring Yuen Woo-ping to choreograph the fight scenes in *The Matrix* (1999). *The Matrix* won four academy awards, made $460m in the global box office, and is considered by many to be one of the best movies of all time.

In the 2000s, epics like *Crouching Tiger, Hidden Dragon*,*Hero, House of Flying Daggers*, and comedies like *Kung Fu Hustle* and *Shaolin Soccer* were heavily influenced by Lee's movies. Lee's influence on director Quentin Tarantino is well documented. Tarantino pays homage to Lee in his choice of outfit for Uma Thurman's character in *Kill Bill*. Thurman wears the same iconic yellow jumpsuit Lee wears in *The Game of Death* during an extended fight scene. It wouldn't be fair to end a rundown of Bruce Lee's influence on cinema without mentioning 2003's *Ong-Bak*. *Ong-Bak* stars Thailand's Tony Jaa, a muay thai fighter whose exceptional skill puts him as close as anyone has ever been to emulating Lee's explosive arrival in Hollywood.

The influence of Lee's movies will never end, as each generation of martial arts filmmakers draws on what came before. *Enter the Dragon* is, and will always be, an exceptional achievement in the history of cinema.

Conclusion

Bruce Lee worked on a total of 46 movies during his career, only six of which were feature movies he starred in as an adult. Lee was in the earliest days of his stardom when he died. It took many years for the world to recognize the trailblazing influence Lee had, not only on martial arts and the movie industry but on the representation of Eastern culture around the world.

Bruce Lee's list of posthumous accolades is endless because it is being added to all the time. Lee was named one of the 100 most influential people of the twentieth century by *Time* magazine. His work has been recognized by the prestigious Asian Awards; Martial Arts Industry Association; the Hong Kong International Film Festival; Housing Boxing Hall of Fame; Ethnic Multicultural Media Academy and many others. Lee even received a congressional tribute from The United States House of Representatives.

Lee's obituary published in the *New York Times* on the day of his death demonstrates the high-brow condescension leveled at Lee's work during his life. The eight-sentence obituary takes the opportunity to say that although Lee's movies were successful in New York, they received unanimously disproving reviews. The obituary also quotes Vincent Canby, a *New York Times* film critic, saying "movies like *Fist of Fury* make 'the worst Italina (sic) Western look like the most solemn and notable achievements of the early Soviet cinema.'"

The *New York Times* attempted to rectify this mean-spirited obituary in 2000 when they revisited Lee's life and legacy and wrote another, fuller obituary. Referring to Lee as a "fighter's fighter," this obituary offers facts about his childhood and martial arts career saying, "Lee's precise, powerful yet seemingly effortless grace and presence before the camera made him an international star." Written almost thirty years apart, the disparity between these accounts of Bruce Lee's influence shows what a huge mistake it was to underestimate Lee Jun-fan, the child whose name promised he would "return again."

Printed in Great Britain
by Amazon

39787011R00030